John Nicholson

The Tennessee Massacre and its Causes

Or, The Utah conspiracy: a lecture delivered in the Salt Lake Theatre, on Monday,

September 22, 1884

John Nicholson

The Tennessee Massacre and its Causes
Or, The Utah conspiracy: a lecture delivered in the Salt Lake Theatre, on Monday, September 22, 1884

ISBN/EAN: 9783743407879

Manufactured in Europe, USA, Canada, Australia, Japa

Cover: Foto ©ninafisch / pixelio.de

Manufactured and distributed by brebook publishing software (www.brebook.com)

John Nicholson

The Tennessee Massacre and its Causes

THE
TENNESSEE MASSACRE

AND

ITS CAUSES;

OR,

THE UTAH CONSPIRACY,

A LECTURE BY

JOHN NICHOLSON, 1839-1909

DELIVERED IN THE SALT LAKE THEATRE;

ON MONDAY, SEPTEMBER 22, 1884.

—————

STENOGRAPHICALLY REPORTED BY JOHN IRVINE.

—————

PRINTED AT JUVENILE INSTRUCTOR OFFICE,

SALT LAKE CITY, UTAH.

1884.

INTRODUCTORY.

THE circumstances which led to the giving of this lecture in the Salt Lake Theatre are as follows:

Mr. Nicholson, by special request of Bishop H. B. Clawson, delivered an address under a similar title in the Twelfth Ward Assembly Rooms, on the 14th of September, 1884. The impression created by it was such as to result in the annexed correspondence:

SALT LAKE CITY,
September 17, 1884.

John Nicholson, Esq.,

DEAR SIR:—The address delivered by you on the 14th inst , in the Twelfth Ward Assembly Rooms. on the subject of the recent massacre of "Mormon" Elders in Tennessee, and the causes which led to that fearful tragedy, having created a deep interest in the community, and a desire on the part of very many who were prevented from being present upon that occasion to hear the facts you have in your possession, we, the undersigned, being of the opinion that a more widespread understanding of the circumstances which surround this tragedy, and which led to its perpetration will be of public benefit, respectfully request that you repeat the lecture, or deliver one of a similar nature at as early a date as will be convenient to you.

Upon receiving an intimation from you that a compliance with our request will be agreeable to you, and the date that will be convenient to you to give the lecture, we will take the necessary steps to secure a larger building than the Twelfth Ward Assembly Rooms, and to give suitable notice to the public.

Very respectfully,

Wm. Jennings, Theo. McKean, A. Miner, Francis Cope, Geo. Swan, Heber M. Wells, James Dunn, H. Dinwoodey, G. M. Ottinger, S. W. Sears, David James, G. E. Bourne, John Clark, Elias Morris, Thos. G. Webber and others.

To the Hon. Wm. Jennings and others.

    GENTLEMEN:—In response to your request that I should deliver, in some large hall to be secured by you for the purpose, an address similar to that lately given in the Twelfth Ward Assembly Rooms, I have to say that, although personally reluctant to place myself so conspicuously before the public, I will endeavor to comply with your wish. I suggest Monday night, Sept. 22nd, as suitable for the occasion, if that time is agreeable with your convenience.

Yours respectfully,
JOHN NICHOLSON.

Salt Lake City, Sept. 17th, 1884.

SALT LAKE CITY,
September 18, 1884.

John Nicholson, Esq.,

    DEAR SIR:—Referring to your response of yesterday, wherein you express a willingness to repeat your lecture on the "Tennessee Massacre and Causes Leading Thereto," or one of a similar nature, the business of securing a suitable hall having been considered, we beg to state that we have obtained the Salt Lake Theatre for Monday evening, Sept. 22nd, for that purpose.

Very respectfully,

William Jennings, H. Dinwoodey, David James, Thomas G. Webber, A. Miner, John Clark and others.

THE APPEARANCE OF THE THEATRE.

The appearance of the Theatre on the occasion is thus described by Mr. O. F. Whitney, of the *Deseret News:*

"Probably the most densely packed audience ever within the walls of the Salt Lake Theatre, was seen there last evening at the lecture of Mr. John Nicholson on the 'Tennessee Massacre and its Causes.' The doors were thrown open at 7 o'clock, as announced, and an eager multitude at once thronged into the building. By the time the lecture was to begin, 8 o'clock, it is safe to say that there was not a seat left untaken, and hundreds were standing up, not alone in the lower part of the house, but in every circle as well. It was truly a magnificent sight.

"Nor did the stage present a less splendid appearance. As soon as the curtain rose, as it did promptly on the hour, it was discovered that there was a second audience facing the one which crammed the auditorium. Manager Clawson, who is an adept at such things, had caused the whole stage to be shut in, with the exception of entrances at the wings and rear, with handsome scenery, while the entire available space was filed with chairs, all of them taken, and many more would-be occupants left standing. No less than three or four hundred people were on the stage alone. The surprise awakened at the sight found vent in a burst of applause from those in front. Before this, however, the Theatre Orchestra, under Professor Thomas, who were in their accustomed place, had rendered some nice selections, and the Sixteenth Ward Band, in full uniform, upon the stage, between the curtain and footlights, had supplemented the same with repeated executions in like excellent style."

HON. WILLIAM JENNINGS

then approached the footlights and said: Ladies and gentlemen: before introducing the lecturer, I would like to say that there has been a report on the street this afternoon that there would be a cry of fire made here to-night, to disturb this audience. If such a thing should occur as a cry of fire, I hope you will take no notice of it, but keep your seats and all will be right.

I take pleasure, ladies and gentlemen, in introducing to you Mr. John Nicholson, who will lecture upon "The Tennessee Massacre and Its Causes." [Applause.]

MR. NICHOLSON

stepped forward and was received with loud applause. He then delivered the following

LECTURE.

STENOGRAPHICALLY REPORTED BY JNO. IRVINE.

Mr. Chairman, ladies and gentlemen: the chairman has already announced the subject upon which I propose to treat;

therefore, it is unnecessary for me to repeat it. As you may well suppo e, it is no small matter for a man to occupy the position that I do to-night before this vast audience. I trust that you will bear with me in patience until I shall concentrate my thoughts upon the task that lies before me.

The subject, you will at once admit, is one of absorbing interest, not only to this community of which we form a part, but it has created an interest all over this nation and many other parts of the world besides. Perhaps before proceeding to the discussion of the causes that produced the horrible massacre which sent a thrill through this entire community, and also caused a feeling of regret among all good and upright people who have learned the details of the murder—it would be well, in the first place, to give a brief

NARRATIVE OF THE TRAGEDY

itself. As is the custom with the Elders of the "Mormon" Church, Elders W. S. Berry and Henry Thompson, who were laboring as missionaries in the State of Tennessee, and more especially in Lewis County of that State, made an appointment to hold a meeting and preach their views to the people. That meeting was appointed for 11 o'clock, on the 10th day of August, 1884, at the house of James Condor, on Cane Creek, Lewis County, Tennessee. A short time previous to the filling of that appointment, the Elders whom I have named were unexpectedly joined by two others, Elders John H. Gibbs and William H. Jones.   On the day appointed, three of the Elders—with Elder Jones excepted, he being at the house of Mr. Garrett, a short distance from the Condor farm—assembled at Mr. Condor's habitation and engaged in preliminary exercises, such as the singing of religious hymns and preparing their minds for the devotions in which they were shortly to engage.

Elder Jones, at Mr. Garrett's house, was engaged in reading a discourse of one of the authorities of the "Mormon" Church, for the instruction and edification of a number of people who had assembled there. After he had concluded this, he immediately started on his way to join the others

who were at Condor's; but while he was traversing that short
distance, suddenly a mob of men, in fantastic garbs and
masked faces, and armed and equipped with deadly weapons
for the commission of violence, rushed upon him and made
him a prisoner. Suffice it to say, without entering into the
details so far as he is concerned, for you are more or less
familiar with them, he was left in charge of one of this
armed party, and that guard that was left over him received
instructions from his brother mobocrats that he should, on the
first intimation of any attempt to escape, shoot him down like
a dog—that he should be murdered. You are already aware
that Elder Jones, by the consent and connivance of his guard,
escaped and survives, and has returned to his home and his
friends in Utah.

On leaving Elder Jones, the mob proceeded to the house
of Mr. Condor. They found the proprietor of the place standing by the gate. They made him a prisoner. James Condor
knew the business of that mob who had come with covered
faces armed to the teeth. He knew that they had come to
take the lives of the Elders from Utah, and in order that
these Elders might be defended he called to his boys who
were in the garden—his son and step-son—to go and get their
guns to defend the lives of these men who were under his
protection because under his roof. After the seizure of James
Condor, David Hinson, who appeared to be the leader of the
mob, entered the house where Elder Gibbs was engaged in
selecting texts of scripture for the purpose of enabling him
to preach the doctrines that are taught in the Bible. He took
a gun that was hanging upon the hooks down from over the
back door, and with that weapon, in cold blood, shot Elder
Gibbs down—murdered him! Next this deadly weapon was
presented at Henry Thompson, whose life he also sought.
Elder Berry being close at hand—a man of indomitable
courage and powerful nerve—desirous of saving his brother,
seized the weapon and held it as if it were in the grip of a
vise, and turned it away from the person of his fellow mis-
sionary. At the same moment Elder Berry observed others
of the mobocrats enter the front door with their weapons

leveled upon him, and when he saw that, and feeling that
his doom was sealed, he simply bowed his head and received
the bullets of the assassins in his body and fell dead at their
feet. ·Elder Thompson saw that to remain longer was to
needlessly sacrifice another life, and therefore he made his
escape. As he passed out of the house and was leaving it his
life would have been taken also, only there intervened betwixt
him and the would-be assassin the person of a lady who
passed out of the house and was about to lift her child from
the ground, and Elder Thompson escaped to the woods. In
the meantime, Martin Condor, the son of James Condor,
entered the house and engaged in a struggle with David Hinson for the possession of the weapon that he held, and while
engaged in this struggle some other members of the mob shot
him down and murdered him. In the meantime, J. R. Hud-
son, the step-son of James Condor, entered and leaped up into
the loft of the house to procure a gun, and descended as quick
as thought, almost. He was seized at the foot of the stairs by
two of the murderous ruffians but tearing himself loose he
shot and killed David Hinson, and then he in turn was slain
also, making five dead men, four whose blood was guiltless,
and one of the guilty murderers, who went into eternity with
the blood of innocence upon his hands.

Not satisfied with their diabolical work, thus far, these
fiends incarnate, before leaving the premises, as an after-piece
to the tragedy, poured a volley through the window, a number
of the missiles of death entering and severely wounding the
person of an innocent woman, Mrs. Condor, the mother of the
two murdered boys, and the balance of the bullets entered the
dead body of W. S. Berry.

A CONSPIRACY IN UTAH.

You will agree with me that this was horrible work, and
that those upon whom rests any degree of responsibility for
its consummation have a great deal to answer for. It is my
purpose to show where at least a portion of that responsibility
lies. I think before we get through to-night, that it will be
clearly shown that there exists in Utah, a conspiracy against

the peace, and good order, and well-being of the great majority of the people who inhabit this fair Territory, and that that conspiracy has its headquarters in Salt Lake City. I propose to give you the evidence, and I do not propose to be one-sided in its production, for the conspirators shall furnish it themselves.

On the 7th day of May, 1882, in the Methodist Church of Salt Lake City, I attended a meeting. It was a gathering of rather an unusual character. It was one among ten thousand meetings; so the presiding genius there—the Rev. L. A. Rudisill—stated; for that particular 7th day of May, 1882, had been set aside and consecrated for the purpose of working up a prejudice against the "Mormon" community—of inflaming the minds of the people of this nation against an innocent people who dwell in this Territory.

But I wish you to understand that it was not altogether or purely a religious meeting. It was also political. There is a great deal said in this community, by certain parties, about the amalgamation of church and state. It is very objectionable to them, except, of course, when they engage in it themselves; then it is perfectly right. The conspiracy to which I now allude, is not only of a religious character, but also political. There was there in all his bloom, His Excellency, Governor Eli H. Murray, Judge John R. McBride, Judge Jacob S. Boreman, and Mr. J. F. Bradley. They represented, in that particular instance, the political wing of the conspiracy—Mr. Rudisill and his co-religionist associates the religious wing.

In speaking to the audience assembled on that occasion, Mr. Rudisill stated that the Methodists had always occupied the front rank in opposing "Mormonism," and that principally through the operations of that denomination of religion Congress was *compelled* to pass the Edmunds law. Note the word *compelled*. My memory does not fail me in regard to the details of that meeting. He said *compelled*. But the Edmunds law, he said, was not sufficient for the purpose in view.

His Excellency, the Governor, stated that the Edmunds law was a step in the right direction, but it was far from being satisfactory.

Judge John R. McBride stated that on that particular occasion he felt as if he was an excellent Methodist. [Laughter and applause.]   It is generally understood in the community I believe, that he is no religionist of any kind.   He has a perfect right to take that position, and every man has a right of this kind, be the position what it may.   But in one particular John R. McBride seems to conform somewhat to scriptural requirements; for it has been said by Paul that we should "be all things to all men." [Applause] It appears that this conspirator is willing to be a devout Methodist, or anything else, so long as he can accomplish the object nearest his heart—suppression of "Mormonism"—[applause] or rather the taking away of the political power out of the hands of the majority of the people of Utah, for that is the political part of the conspiracy.   He further stated that in order to reach the "Mormons," one legal provision, especially, should be eliminated from the statute books—that provision which prevents a woman from testifying against her husband.   He also had the effrontery in that meeting to say that he felt that he would make an excellent prosecutor of the "Mormon" Church if he were appointed to that office.   [Applause and laughter.] It does not need a very great change to insert the correct word, and make it *persecutor* of the "Mormon" Church. [Laughter].

Mr. Boreman, or rather Judge Boreman—I hope he will pardon me for forgetting his title—[laughter and applause] when I consider how little he is entitled to it, I think it is very pardonable.   I cannot tell you very well what Judge Boreman did say, it was so absurd.   He seemed to be in a passion—worked up to a remarkable degree.   He said something about the people who belonged to the "Mormon" Church in England desiring to proclaim Brigham Young king, and a lot of nonsense of that kind.   If anybody had asked me what I thought about his speech on that occasion when the religious and political conspirators met together, I should have been much inclined to have given the same description that was given by a student when he was asked to state his opinion of a speech of a fellow student. He said it was "an heterogeneous. concatenation of extraneous phraseology." [Laughter and applause.]

Mr. 'Bradley did not make out much better in this connection than our friend, Mr. Boreman. His speech was about as unintelligible; it was not edifying, especially to me, although I was glad I was present for your sakes, ladies and gentlemen, who were not there, that I might tell you what took place.

There are some others whom I wish to bring to your attention, for I desire to show you to-night that there has been a systematic, determined purpose put in operation, to spread through this country, as far as their influence could reach, the most infamous, scandalous fabrications that could possibly be conceived in the brains of human beings, that under cover of a prejudice thus created, the design of the conspirators might be accomplished.

I draw your attention to the case of the Rev. R. G. McNiece, who is very anxious about the welfare of this community; exceedingly so. Not very long since he presented in the *Independent*, a very influential journal published in the East, his views, or what purported to be his views, on the "Mormon" question, and you may be sure he did not wish to paint the "Mormon" community in favorable colors. He wanted to make the impression upon the country, through the medium of the *Independent*, that the "Mormons" are a lawless, murderous, vile community of wretches, that should not be permitted to live. As evidence that they should be robbed of their rights, or that all political power should be taken away from them, he stated that his fellow religionists in Utah had been placed in great jeopardy through the buildings that they occupied and their churches being stoned and set on fire, and in consequence of this the lives, these valuable lives, of himself and fellow religionists had been placed in jeopardy. Of course it was the "Mormons" who committed these outrages.

When his attention was drawn to his perfidy through a public journal of this city, he cited a number of alleged instances to sustain the statements which he had made. But before I proceed any further, I wish to say now that his statements in the *Independent* were endorsed by some of the political conspirators, Judge Rosborough, Judge Jacob S. Boreman and one of the editors of the *Salt Lake Tribune*, Colonel Nelson, for the chief editor was at that time in Washington, supposedly for the purpose, under cover of the prejudice already created against the "Mormons," of procuring legislation to rob the "Mormons" of their political rights. I think that any statement made by the Rev. McNiece certainly needs endorsing [laughter] as I propose to show. He cited as an instance of his truthfulness that about eighteen months previous, in the city of Logan, an attempt had been made to burn the Presbyterian Church of that town. The facts in regard to that circumstance were these: On the 30th day of November, 1882, a church sociable was held in that building, the Rev. Mr. Parks presiding, and there broke in upon the harmony of the occasion an individual by the name of William Buder, a non-"Mormon," and presumably a member of the "liberal" party. He was in a state of beastly intoxication. He desired to be admitted into this church sociable, and forced his way into the building. The Rev. Mr. Parks, who seems to believe a little in muscular Christianity—and I do not blame him—took him neck and crop and bundled him out [applause] just as he should have done. But William Buder, a non-"Mormon," said to the Rev. Parks, "I'll get even with you." On that same night, at a late hour, an attempt was made to set the building on fire, and the subsequent investigation, according to all the circumstances discoverable after a close scrutiny, pointed to William Buder as the would-be incendiary. Mr. Parks believed it was William Buder, a non-"Mormon," who had sought in that way to get even with him, and so did everybody else familiar with the facts, and I do not know but what Mr. McNiece was just as familiar with the details as anybody else; presumably so, for no honorable gentleman will attempt to give publicity to any important circumstance involving the good character of his fellowmen, unless he is first satisfied of the truthfulness of his position by a candid investigation. [Applause.] But don't you see that to have stated that William Buder, a non-"Mormon," was the incendiary would have spoiled the object, for the crime must be placed upon the broad shoulders of the Latter-day Saints? [Applause.] It must be shown that they are lawless, and that they threatened and endangered the lives of these lambs—in wolves' clothing. [Laughter and applause.]*

Some of the churches are quite remarkable for heroes. Perhaps, ladies and gentlemen, you are not aware of the heroism that has been occasionally exhibited right in your midst. ["No."] Perhaps I might state some instances of such heroism. There was another reverend gentleman, by the name of McMillan, whose diocese was for a time in Sanpete County, Utah: He was treated with great consideration and kindness by the people there. He was given the free use of the meeting house of the "Mormons," in the town of Ephraim, and he was very grateful. You will see the character of his gratitude at a glance when I show you how he returned the courtesy shown him by the savage "Mormons." He went back to the East. What for? Because there is more than one purpose in regard to the defamation of the "Mormon" community. It is naturally to be supposed that these heroes shall make a sensational anti-"Mormon" speech when they go East to facilitate the process of passing around the hat. Therefore he had to make a hero of himself. He made the declaration that in the quiet town of Ephraim, in Sanpete, this remarkably brave man, when he mounted the rostrum had to take in one hand a weapon of death—a revolver—and the word of the Lord in the other [laughter and applause] to protect himself against the lawless "Mormons" who sought his life.

What an absurdity this story bears on it face when you think of it. When he returned he was met or waited upon by

Canute Petersen, one of the leading men of Sanpete County, who spoke to him about his misstatements, and pointed out to him that such fabrications were most infamous. He was very sorry. He was humble. He was very meek. He said he felt as if he had done wrong, but he would make it right just as soon as it was possible. He subsequently paid another visit to the East. How did he make it right? He simply repeated his former statements and added a few more falsehoods to give spice to his story, and his speech was subsequently published in the Denver papers.

But this was a second-hand way of making notoriety; for the Rev. Lyford, who had officiated at Provo, had made himself a hero in the same line. Some of you remember, perhaps, his remarkable hairbreadth escapes; but he always came out alive [laughter and applause] and consequently his own existence furnishes the best evidence of the falsity of his statements. If that gentleman had dropped the latter part of his name and left the first two letters it would have been exactly in keeping with his conduct. [Applause.]

When I was in Ogden in 1881, on July 11th of that year, a committee of a Methodist conference that was held there expressed their views on the "Mormon" question, and what ought to be done with it. Their resolutions were published at the time; they were duly given to a gaping world   Here is an extract from that document:

"Mormonism holds the balance of power in Idaho and Arizona and menaces New Mexico, Colorado, Wyoming and Montana.   We believe polygamy is a foul system of licentiousness, practiced in the name of religion, hence hideous and revolting.   It should not be reasoned with, but ought to be STAMPED OUT."

Fancy that! The "Mormon" religion must not be reasoned with.   Do not bring the magical touchstone of reason to bear upon this question at all, but apply the truly Christian method; let it be "stamped out." [Applause.]   O what a rarity in Christian charity! [Applause.]   Only fancy, if you can, the Savior of the world, and those whom He chose to officiate in connection with Him, speaking to His disciples in reference to the religions that existed in that day, and that were not similar to that which He taught, telling them, "these religions are wrong, they are not right; do not reason with them; they must be 'stamped out.'" And yet these men who met together in Ogden and considered the question of another religion, take the position that that religion, because it does not conform to their ideas, should not be reasoned with, but that it should be "stamped out." What an outrage on common sense and common decency! What a parody on the Christian religion are these men and their views! [Applause.] They also made this political recommendation:

"*Resolved* that it is the sense of this body that the laws of this Territory should be made by a council appointed by the President of the United States and confirmed by the Senate."

This means that every vestige of popular government should be swept away from this Territory and an autocracy established in its place. But you must remember that they are opposed to any interference in any shape whatever of the church with the state—except, of course, when they do it themselves.

I hold in my hand the conspirators' campaign document, "A Handbook on Mormonism," it is called. I call it a production of diabolism; for it is filled with lies and misrepresentations against the "Mormon" people and their religion from beginning to end. I will read you one little extract from the bitter pen of Rev. J. M. Coyner. His name is suggestive. As a *coiner* of falsehoods he is a decided success. [Applause.] There are many "Mormons" present. Listen how this man describes your religion:

"Mormonism is made up of twenty parts. Take eight parts diabolism, three parts of animalism from the Mohammedan system, one part bigotry from old Judaism, four parts cunning and treachery from Jesuitism, two parts Thuggism from India and two parts Arnoldism, and then shake the mixture over the fires of animal passion, and throw in the forms and ceremonies of the Christian religion, and you will have this system in its true component elements."

A professed Christian wrote this, for it is not the policy of men such as he to allow the "Mormons" to describe their own religion. Of course, the Methodists, the Presbyterians and all other denominations would expect that it would be the proper thing to go outside of themselves, and especially to their enemies, for a correct description or explanation of their religious tenets and views. Judging from the way they treat the "Mormons," one would suppose that that would be their idea; to be consistent it would.

But is this campaign document altogether religious? Not by any means. Do not make a mistake by supposing so; for wherever you find the religious wing of the Utah conspiracy, you will find the political wing within short range. Who are the writers of the articles in this book—"The Handbook on Mormonism"—the product of diabolism? I will give you a few of them you are familiar with. The Rev. R. G. McNiece, [laughter] Eli H. Murray, [great laughter and applause] the Rev. J. M. Coyner, Jacob S. Boreman, [laughter and applause] the Rev. T. B. Hilton, J. R. McBride, [laughter] O. J. Hollister [much laughter and applause] and others.

(The lecturer created great merriment by using the plaintive tone commonly used by a priest when he named the clergymen, and vociferating after the manner of a stump speaker when he uttered the name of a political schemer.)

There is another source more prolific of defamation in this community. I refer to the *Salt Lake Tribune*, the organ of the conspirators. I wish that source to furnish some of the evidence to sustain the position that I take to-night. There was published on the 15th day of March, 1884, what was termed "A Red Hot Address." It purported to have been delivered by a "Mormon" Bishop named West, in the little town of Juab in the southern portion of this Territory. It was very prudent to select a little side station; for the discovery of a forgery would not, in the opinion of the conspirators, be so easily made if perpetrated upon a place of that kind. What was the character of that "Red Hot Address," said to have been delivered by a "Mormon" Bishop? It recommended the assassination of those who opposed the "Mormon" community. One of the objects of the wrath of Bishop West was His Excellency Governor Eli H. Murray. And Bishop West told his audience that it was their imperative duty to seize upon His Excellency and tread him down until his bowels gushed out on the streets, and that those who should succeed him, if they did not behave themselves better toward the "Mormon" community than he, should be treated in a similar way. This "Red Hot Address" was true, with a few trifling exceptions. I wish you to note the exceptions; for the organ of the conspirators does not stand upon trifles; not by any means. ["No."] In the first place there is no Bishop West in the "Mormon" Church, and has not been for many years. There was no meeting held in Juab on the day on which that address was said to have been delivered. No address of that kind was ever delivered. With these trifling exceptions the address was entirely correct.* [Laughter and applause.]

I wish you to note .this fact, however, that if there ever were any individuals on the face of this earth susceptible of being deceived, they are the editors of the *Salt Lake Tribune*. They are so innocent, so guileless, so harmless themselves, that they do not think that anybody would do anything wrong. They are remarkable for innocence. Why, a child might deceive them—that is providing—providing they are supplied with something that will scandalize the characters of the "Mormon" community. Then they are easily deceived. Very easily deceived, indeed. So this "Red Hot Address" was a canard. They were very much deceived. They even went so far as to say that they were really imposed upon by some person who furnished that address for publication, and they made an apology. What an apology it was! An apology for an apology. Let me see what kind of an apology they made for this "Red Hot Address," fabricated out of whole cloth. Here is a quotation from the paper of which I am speaking:

"The case of the 'Red Hot Address' has been cited, which was corrected as soon as the managers of this journal found they had been imposed upon."

---

*——See Appendix.

1*

Here is a qualification to that apology quoted from the same sheet:

"There was not a thing in that bogus sermon which has not been taught in the Tabernacle harangues."

What do you think of an apology of that kind? I call that a re-assertion of the fabrication, and the apology is worse than the first falsehood. [Applause.]

I will give you another sample apology for something else; goodness knows what, that appeared in that innocent sheet. Here it is:

"By a mistake a jot appeared in the *Tribune* yesterday, which does not reflect the sentiments of any owner or director of this journal. It was, too, as objectionable in manner as matter. It was altogether wrong; its publication is a matter of pain and mortification to us, and we grieve sincerely that it ever found its way into the *Tribune.*"

Can you tell me to what that refers? What predicament does that leave me and you in, ladies and gentlemen? It leaves you and me in this dilemma, that we must apply that apology to the entire sheet, and you must do that in order to cover the ground. [Laughter and applause.]

We hear it frequently asserted by these journalists, these conspirators—I must not, I suppose, use that word too often, because I might perhaps tread on some of their corns, and I surely would not like to do that; but we are frequently told that these men are "American gentlemen." I think they must be so. We must consider them "American gentlemen," for here is the evidence of it: They have said they are themselves. [Laughter and applause.] According to their own description of themselves I think if Chesterfield were living now he would be ashamed of himself. Gentlemen, of course, are considerate of the feelings of others. They are very delicate about giving offense, and especially avoid speaking in a derogatory way of any sentiment or feeling that is sacred in the breasts of their fellow creatures. "American gentlemen" would never do that.

I call your attention to a portion of the faith of the "Mormon" religion. The "Mormons" believe in the religion that they have espoused, and like other people they have a right to their religious views. They believe that by the performance of vicarious work, the performance by proxy of ordinances by the living for the dead—provided it is accepted by the dead in the spirit world, a saving influence is brought to bear upon those who have passed away from this earth without obedience to the gospel. This is a sacred principle with them. It is so sacred to them, and it is a subject of such absorbing interest to them, that I know of men in the community that have traversed sea and land for thousands of miles for the purpose of gleaning information in regard to their dead relatives, that they might officiate in their stead, and their work here be of some benefit to their progenitors, and, as I have said, their views are sacred to them. Of course no gentleman would hold up their religious views as a subject for vulgar merriment, however much he might differ from them. He would consider them sacred to him because sacred to his fellow-creatures. He would not hold them up to ridicule and make those who entertain them the laughing-stock of the populace. Surely an "American gentleman" would not be guilty of so grave and vulgar a breach of common decency as this. But let us see. I will read an extract from the paper published, managed and conducted by the self-described "American gentlemen":

OFFICIATING FOR THE STIFFS.

"A short time ago a Mormon Saintess went through the Logan Temple and was baptized or sealed to and had adopted into her family thirty dead relatives. It took three days to perform the various ceremonies and ordinations, and no doubt the defunct will now rise from their tombs, or from their HEATED DWELLING places. Her husband contemplates going through a similar ceremony and as he has taken the trouble to look up his genealogy, he has calculated that it will take him exactly four months to perform the sacred rites for the various STIFFS that were once members of his family. The fools are not all dead yet."

And this, ladies and gentleman, emanated from these considerate "American gentlemen." [Applause.] Judge ye of their quality! In the organ of the conspirators there have been slanders most vile. Neither sex nor age has been spared in the vile calumnies that have been heaped upon private individuals. I would not insult this audience by recounting the foul aspersions, the assassin stabs upon private character that have been again and again and again perpetrated in the most shameless manner in that unprincipled sheet published and conducted by the self-described "American gentlemen." [Applause.]

In speaking of the clique that constantly conspires against the commonwealth of Utah, I would not have you suppose that I refer to the bulk of non-Mormons of this Territory, among whom are to be found many honorable people who have no lot nor part in the conspiracy and who do not give it their sympathy. The plot is confined to a comparatively few designing characters, who spare no efforts to whip others into line. The operations of these enemies of liberty in Utah, are, in my opinion, heartily despised by many people who have no connection with the "Mormon" Church, nor sympathy with its doctrines. Even numbers of clergymen take this position.

THE OBJECT OF THE CONSPIRACY.

What has been the object of these vile detractions of an innocent community? Two fold in its character. The religious wing of the conspiracy desires to have the "Mormon" religion crushed out, because in their operations here they have no religious success. Their efforts are barren and unfruitful. They stay here and go back eastward when they wish to pass around the hat. They return after getting the financial benefits of their vile calumnies and giving descriptions of their personal heroism and hairbreadth escapes among the lawless "Mormons." They are hirelings. They preach for hire and divine for money. The Elders of the "Mormon" Church are a standing reproach to such men. Like the immediate followers of Him whom they profess to serve, they go out into the world without purse or scrip, as they did, and they have success in their labors. When they go they take their lives in their hands as those men did who were brutally murdered on Cane Creek, Lewis County. Tennessee; and when they return they bring their sheaves with them. And in this way a religious, honest and industrious community is built up in the Territory of Utah and adjacent places in this part of the great West. The success of these Elders is a standing reproach to the hirelings who have no success in their labors, and therefore they want that reproach wiped out, or, according to the priests who assembled in Ogden, they desire that "Mormonism" should not be *reasoned* with but *stamped out.* This is the object of the religious wing of this conspiracy. When the Elders go abroad they have a great deal to meet. For instance I will explain what they have had to encounter in western and middle Tennessee, where the Elders who were slain on Cane Creek were laboring. What was the situation before that horrible tragedy was consummated? Everywhere they went, they had presented to them the "Red Hot Address," published in this city by the organ of the conspirators. It was specially handed about and circulated by a Baptist preacher named Vandever, of Hohenwald, Lewis County. I have the facts here [holding up a letter in his hand]* giving names and details from one of the survivors of the massacre on Cane Creek—Elder W. H. Jones. It has been said that there has been no evidence of the "Red Hot Address" ever having gone to Tennessee. Not only was that "Red Hot Address" there, but Elder Gibbs who was slain, and Elder Jones who survives, presented to this Baptist preacher whom I have named a refutation of the slanderous fabrication, in order that he might redress the evil that he had accomplished by its dissemination among the people, and which had inflamed the minds of the populace to such an extent that they were prepared largely by that statement or alleged address purporting to have been delivered by a "Mormon" bishop, to shed the blood of the Elders, and they did it; and

---

*——EXTRACT FROM ELDER JONES' LETTER.—"This villainous, slanderous fabrication was circulated over the country. Parson Vandever worked up prejudice against us in that section by giving it [the 'Red Hot Address'] wide publicity, and by his pretended credence to the falsehood, causing great excitement. Elder Gibbs and I sent by mail to Vandever an exposure of the address in question, but he did not show it to anybody that we know of."

the blood of innocence is upon the skirts of those who perpetrated that infamy. The authorship of an indirect cause of
the murder is now traced home to them; they cannot relieve
themselves of it.

What is the other part of the conspiracy? The "Mormons"
are in the majority here, and as the majority rules everywhere
in this republic, as a natural consequence they hold the balance of political power in the Territory. And the infamous
lies, some of which I have recounted, that have been spread
far and wide to show that the "Mormons" are a lawless people, that they are a vile people, that they are not fit to live,
were intended to form a prejudice in the minds of the people
throughout the country generally, in order that the conspirators might operate under that feeling with impunity. They
imagined that but few if any people in the nation, in the light
or face of existing prejudice thus created, would think they
were doing wrong. This part of the conspiracy is to sweep
away from Utah every vestige of popular rule and concentrate
the political power in the hands of an unscrupulous few, or in
the hands of what I call the office-seekers' combination of
Utah—those who are hungry for office and its spoils—that
they might grind the "Mormon" community into the dust.
I will give you the proof, and the other side shall supply the
evidence:

In November, 1880, an election was held in this Territory
for a delegate to Congress from Utah. The candidate of the
People's Party was the Hon. George Q. Cannon, the candidate of the conspirators Mr. Allen G. Campbell. The Hon.
George Q. Cannon received of the popular vote on that occasion considerable over 18,000 votes, and Allen G. Campbell
about 1,300. Did this express the popular will? In what
more forcible way can the popular will be exhibited than by
the franchise? It was the duty of His Excellency, Governor
Eli H. Murray, to furnish the candidate who received the
largest number of votes a certificate to that effect, to present
as a credential in the House of Representatives, and he gave
that certificate to the man that received 1,300 votes. Does

that not prove, as far as it goes, the character of the conspiracy? It is to usurp the political authority that belongs to the people in a republican form of government. He who gave that certificate, certified to a falsehood, and made an attempt to dethrone the power of the people, to thwart the public will, the popular will, and establish his will, an autocracy, and to wrest from the people the reins of government.

I will still further show the political character of the conspiracy, and also why so many infamous lies have been told about the "Mormons," that under cover of these falsehoods and the prejudice resulting, the objects of this conspiracy might be attained.

On the 3rd day of August, 1882, there was inserted in the sundry civil appropriation bill, in Congress, an amendment made by Senator Hoar. It was offered in view of the fact that through the negligence of the Utah Commission the election that ought to have occurred in that month lapsed. The amendment thus inserted was passed there, giving authority to His Excellency, Eli H. Murray, to fill all vacancies that might occur in offices in this Territory through the lapse of that election that should have been held. Fortunately, however, there is a Territorial statute which provides that in case of any deficiency in regard to filling the offices by the lapse of an election, or through any other cause, such as an intended successor to an ffioce not qualifying within statutory time, the incumbent should hold over until such time as a legal election should take place; and therefore there were no vacancies. So it was held pretty generally even by those that were very prominent, subsequently, on the other side. I might be allowed to state here that it is publicly known that Mr. Marshall, a prominent lawyer of this city, stated that there were no vacancies, and he so expressed himself to quite a number of persons belonging to the People's Party. However, passing that over I now direct your attention to the fact that there were a large number of offices that were not vacant in any case, the election to which could not legally have occurred for a year subsequent to that August election. But the party who desired to make the seizure of the political power of

Utah do not stand upon trifles; His Excellency. Eli H. Murray, in the face of these facts, endeavored to fill nearly every office in Utah Territory by his appointment, and in that way overthrow every vestige of popular rule in Utah Territory. This was an evidence of the impatience of the office hunters' party, because they anticipated by this act the legislation which they desired on that subject. Much anxiety has been manifested by certain persons whom I have named in regard to the political affairs of this Territory. Among the officers—among these would-be officers—appointees of the governor, were found some of the gentlemen who figured conspicuously in the first meeting in the Methodist Church, the details of which I have already furnished this audience. Judge Jacob S. Boreman was gubernatorially appointed to an office in this county; also Mr. J. F. Bradley. It is a wonder that Judge J. R. McBride was left out in the cold; but there was nothing large enough, I presume, to satisfy that gentleman. [Laughter.]

Have I not proven to a demonstration the object of this conspiracy, and the reason why such infamous fabricated statements are sent abroad to prejudice the minds of the people against the "Mormon" community? I think that I have, and I have taken the evidence from the other side of the fence. They have furnished the proof themselves, and I have only made use of it.

EFFECTS OF THE CONSPIRACY UPON CONGRESS.

What are the effects of this conspiracy and this prejudice upon Congress? The effects are these: Laws that we consider to be unconstitutional are introduced into Congress and some of them are passed and become law. For instance there is the Edmunds law with which you are all more or less familiar. One of its chief objects was to disfranchise those who were practical polygamists in the "Mormon" community, and that was effectually done in the operation of that law. But some men have India rubber consciences, and they injected this India rubber material into the law and made it stretch. The Utah Commission—I talk respectfully of that body of gentlemen—made that law stretch to its utmost capacity.

They almost went outside of polygamy altogether. If they had just gone half an inch further they would have excluded from the polls persons who were first cousins to polygamists. [Applause and laughter.] There is one very peculiar feature associated with the Edmunds law. There has been introduced in connection with its operations, without the color or authority of law, a test oath. That oath made its first appearance, I think, in 1879—if my memory serves me correctly—in what was known as the Willits' bill, a measure that was introduced into Congress, but did not pass. It was formulated—so I have been given to understand—by the Utah conspirators here and furnished to Mr. Willits to be incorporated in his Utah bill. It was subsequently used by His Excellency, Eli H. Murray, and had to be subscribed to by every person elected to any office in this Territory before he could receive a commission. And now, under the Edmunds law, every person who walks up to the registrar's office to register has to take this iron-clad oath, a copy of which I now hold in my hand. If I had been a conspirator I do not think that I should have favored the introduction of this particular oath. My reason for this is that, according to a vulgarism, it "gives the whole thing away." I will not read the entire oath, but will read a portion of it: "That I have not lived or cohabited with more than one woman *in the marriage relation.*" [The lecturer's manner of uttering the words in italics in a subdued tone created great laughter and applause.] That oath makes a wide opening through which the corruptionist, steeped up to his neck in filth and crime can crawl [loud applause] and builds around the man who conscientiously enters more or less into the marriage relation a wall deep, thick and high, so that he cannot get through or climb over. Does not that give the thing away? I am not displeased that they formulated that oath. It shows the position exactly. It exhibits the superiority of the "Mormon" community over the corruptionists. [Applause.]

There is a custom whenever a man comes into special prominence in political matters for his admirers to wear a particular kind of hat. For instance, there is the Cleveland hat, and there is the Blaine hat. I have a recommendation to offer to the conspirators, and why not adopt it?　　Let us have an "anti-marriage relation hat." [Applause,] Let it be of spotless white, emblematical of the purity of the characters of those entitled to wear it [laughter] and let there be written in gold letters—large, so they can be easily read by the passing observer—the words: "I HAVE NOT LIVED NOR CO-HABITED WITH MORE THAN ONE WOMAN," and in small letters [applause and laughter] so that you can hardly see them, "In the marriage relation." [Renewed applause and laughter.] The saving clause should be very obscure, it tells such a horrible tale.

In the anti-"Mormon" crusade first meeting, details of which I have given, Judge McBride said that he desired that that legal provision which prevented a woman from testifying against her husband should be expunged from the statute books, and you can see the ear-marks of the Utah conspirators in all the legislation that has been introduced into Congress.　I am not here to blame the national legislators for what they have done, for I believe it has been largely the result of the misrepresentations that have been made by the conspirators whose head quarters are in this city.　They have acted in the belief that the "Mormon" community were as vile as they have been painted by these, I was going to say —— you can imagine—I do not wish to use anything but respectful language, because I am speaking of "American gentlemen." [Applause.]　And what is the character of the crusade legislation?　One of the first provisions of the Hoar amendment act passed by the Senate at its last session, provides that the wife shall testify against the husband, and as the husband and the wife are one, the monstrous doctrine is incorporated that a man shall be compelled to testify, in that sense, against himself.　What an outrage to attempt to demolish a leading safeguard which maintains the sacredness of the family circle!　Shame on the instigators of such legislation!　I have a right to express my sentiments regarding so flagrant an outrage sought to be perpetrated upon an innocent people.

This law also proposes, in certain cases, that a witness shall be treated as a criminal by abolishing the ordinary process of the subpœna and providing that an attachment shall issue.

And the "Mormon" community, according to this remarkable measure, shall have no power to transact their own secular
business, but it proposes to perform it for them by fourteen
trustees appointed by the President of the United States. It
is a wonder that they did not incorporate some provision in the
law that Bishop Preston and his Counselors of the "Mormon"
Church should be deposed from their positions—it amounts to
nearly the same thing—and that a Bishop and Counselors be
appointed by the President of the United States [laughter].

Further, the franchise is, according to this law, to be swept
away from the ladies. What an ungallant lot these conspirators are! Operating against the ladies whom they claim
are in bondage in Utah, and yet they want to take an un-
warrantable step to enslave them politically.

It further provides that the property of the "Mormons" shall
be confiscated summarily; and that under no pretence whatever shall the people amalgamate for the purpose of bringing
people to this Territory from abroad. Therefore, if this were
law—let us hope for the sake of republican institutions that
it never will be—you would not have the privilege of bringing
to this land your father, or your grandmother, or your cousins,
or your aunt, or any of your relatives, *because they are "Mormons."*

What a parody on legislation!—the result of the work of a
conspiracy, religious and political, in the Territory of Utah,
with its headquarters in Salt Lake City. That is the character of the legislation sought to be brought about by that combination, to sweep away the liberties of the people and grasp
the power that will grind them into the dust, under the cover
of the prejudice that they have created by their infamous
falsehoods.

ATTITUDE OF THE CONSPIRATORS SINCE THE MASSACRE.

I will now show the position that has been taken by representatives of the conspiracy since the massacre took place,
that unhappy and horrible deed in Lewis County, Tennessee.
There is, I believe, a general understanding that the chief
editor of the *Tribune* is or has been a member of the legal

profession. He is called Judge Goodwin. I do not know how far that goes. I presume that if I was to say to this audience, for the purpose of receiving an answer, "How do you do, Colonel?" there would by a chorus of voices, there are so many colonels in this country. And so it is with judges. But I believe that the gentleman I now speak of possesses legal knowledge. What an unfortunate thing that he does not inject it into his journalism!

Here is a quotation embodying another quotation, which the *Tribune* in its issue of Sep. 16th, 1884, contains:

"On the other hand, the reason why the violence was committed has been boldly given. The clergyman of Nashville, extracts of whose sermon we gave last week, openly says:"

"'The law-abiding citizens charge upon these Mormon missionaries that, under the guise of religion, they were attempting to seduce their wives and daughters from the paths of virtue, and they have not disproved it.'"

"We have other evidence of the same kind."

Were Judge Goodwin on the bench instead of the tripod, and he should take a similar position in regard to charges made against alleged law-breakers brought before him, what would be the result? Suppose a man was charged with murder in his court, and the jury were asked to bring in a verdict, his instructions after the trial would be something like this: "You must bring in a verdict of guilty, for this man is charged with murder, and has not disproved it." What a remarkable position to be taken by an intelligent man! According to his position all you have to do in order to prove a person guilty is to make a charge against him, and convict him providing he fails to disprove it. That is reversing the usual methods of justice with a vengeance. These Elders were charged by the local priests whose prejudices, probably, were incited by the "Red Hot Address" and other documents of that description—with attempting to seduce the wives and daughters of citizens of Tennessee, and they have not disproved it. What a travesty on common sense! How absurd! How ridiculous! But then they have other evidence—proof—of the same kind. They have evidence to the effect

that charges have been made against these Elders, and these
Elders have not disproved it. Very remarkable that they
have not disproved it seeing that they are dead! What a
wonderful thing to take place in our day, that these men,
murdered in cold blood, because charges have been made
against them to palliate the crime perpetrated by the murderers, and because they do not rise out of their graves, to
which they were sent by the hands of assassins before their
time, to disprove the charges, they must be guilty! How
supremely ridiculous!

After the murder was perpetrated all the respect that could
be shown by a grief-stricken community was exhibited to
those who were ruthlessly slain. Their remains were buried
by those who survived that awful tragedy near the spot where
their blood was shed. Elder B. H. Roberts, and others, at
the risk of their lives, proceeded to the place where they were
entombed and exhumed the bodies and prepared them to be
dispatched to their sorrowing relatives, as the last grain of
comfort that could be given to the bereaved. I said these
men performed this brotherly act at the risk of their lives, as
was subsequently proved. On their return trip from Cane
Creek they lost their way. Happily for them that they did;
for there was a party of mobbers ambushed ready to shed their
blood also, even when they were on this mission of mercy and
brotherly kindness. However, the bodies were brought here.
The remains of Elder Berry were taken to the South, to Ka-
narra and consigned to his family, and the remains of Elder
Gibbs to Paradise, his home when he was alive. And throughout this Territory, and in every place where the news had
reached the "Mormons," arrangements were made to hold
services in honor of the dead, to show the respect of the
people for those who had been slain. Among these meetings
was a large assemblage in the Tabernacle of this city, which
was crowded on the occasion; an immense host convened there,
and certain Elders poured out their thoughts in words of
respect for the dead and grief for the awful act that had caused
the death of these men.

But more eloquently still was the prevailing sentiment expressed by the moistened eyes which could be seen all over that vast congregation, so far as the faces came distinctly within the range of vision of the observer.

What was the position taken by the organ of the conspirators, the Salt Lake *Tribune*, regarding these solemn ceremonies? That sheet contained, in its following issue, an alleged description, of the proceedings, and it was a travesty—a farce. What think you of men who can be so lost to the better feelings of humanity that they can take the grief, the sorrow of their fellow creatures and laughingly gloat over and hold it up as something to be vulgarly joked about? I say that the degradation of the human heart cannot reach a lower depth than that [applause], and I say that men who can be guilty of such an outrage are lost to all of the better feelings of humanity [applause]. Perhaps you think I speak strongly on this subject. I want you to understand that I speak no more strongly than I feel [applause].

Perhaps there may be some in the audience that think an apology is due from me for my severity. I feel that my apology must be of a similar character to that which was given by a member of the British House of Parliament, when he was guilty of making some personal remarks regarding a member of that august body. He was called upon for an apology; he remarked: "I said the gentleman on the other side was a scoundrel, and I am sorry for it." He was sorry he was a scoundrel [laughter and applause]. I have stated that men who are guilty of such outrages as those which I have described are lost to all that makes man noble, and I am sorry for it—I am sorry they are so lost [applause].

It appears that the surviving Elders in Tennessee, B. H. Roberts and others, petitioned Governor Bate of that State to take official steps to have the murderers arrested and punished for the fearful crime. In response, this magnanimous governor offered the munificent sum of $1,000 to be spread over a whole crowd of mobbers and murderers. But the sum seemed exceedingly large to His Excellency Governor Eli H. Murray. Doubtless he thought it vastly too much. He sent to Governor Bate a dispatch of congratulation. He stated in that dispatch that he was glad to see that Governor Bate was taking some steps to have those who killed the Elders brought to justice, because it was no just reason that they should be murdered because they were agents of "organized crime." What do you think the governor sent that dispatch for? He was overwhelmed with hypocritical grief. He, under cover of this pretended sorrow, like the senseless ostrich that thinks when its head is in the sand it cannot be seen, only made other portions of his physical structure appear all the more prominent [laughter and applause]. He sent that dispatch in order to tell the people of Tennessee and the country generally that the Elders who were killed were but the agents of "organized crime;" but—really—of course —it was not exactly the right thing to kill them. But still they were merely agents of "organized crime" [applause]. *

Perhaps you and I may think that the governor stepped out of his way in order to interfere with the affairs of a commonwealth, with which he has no more to do officially or personally than the humblest citizen of this Territory. But, then, how could he get it before the country, that the Elders who were killed were agents of "organized crime" unless he

---

*——Governor Murray's Dispatch—

SALT LAKE CITY,
Aug. 22d.

Gov. W. B. Bate, Nashville, Tenn.:
Dispatches state that you are exerting yourself to vindicate the laws in the matter of the murder of Mormon missionaries in Tennessee. I thank you for this action. The charges of preaching polygamy does not excuse murder. I trust that you may bring the guilty to punishment, thereby preventing such lawlessness in Tennessee or elsewhere. Lawlessness in Tennessee and Utah are alike reprehensible. but the murdered Mormon agents in Tennessee were sent from here as they have been for years by the representatives of organized crime, and I submit that as long as Tennessee's representatives in Congress are, to say the least, indifferent to the punishment of offenders against the national law in Utah, such cowardly outrages by their constituents as the killing of emigration agents sent there from here will continue.

ELI H. MURRAY,
Governor.

should make that interference. It could not be otherwise
done; so excellent an opportunity could not be let slip in order
to create, *to create*, to manufacture the same feeling that
caused the murder of five human beings and the wounding of
an innocent woman. That was all that the dispatch was intended to do, in my opinion.

But do you think that the governor sent that dispatch of
his own accord and volition altogether? Do you think, now,
honestly, ladies and gentlemen, that he formulated that dispatch and sent it outside of the conspiracy combination? If
you do, then you do not exactly believe the same as I do
[laughter]. I am too familiar with the operations of that small
circle of schemers to believe any such thing. In the first
place my opinion is—when I express an opinion I give it as
such; when I relate facts I sustain them as facts; I give you
this as my opinion, you can take it for what it is worth—it
was first necessary to secure the approval and consent of him
who has said, on the streets of this city, that he is practically
the governor of Utah. Do you know who he is? Patrick
H. Lannan [loud laughter and applause], an American gentleman of Cork [great applause and laughter], or the County
Down, or some other place in equally close proximity to New
York or Massachusets [renewed laughter and applause].
The gentleman whom I have named is given to talking. I
might say very much given to talking. It has been said that
perpetual motion has never been brought to light, but Mr.
Lannan's tongue comes the nearest to it of anything that has
been discovered [laughter and applause]. He has stated that
the governor cannot make any prominent move without he is
consulted in regard to it. He has told this very broadly, and
the information is from his side of the house. This is very
well known, and it rasps a little on the feelings of some of his
own friends. Now, ladies and gentlemen, as the showman
said, "you pays your money and you takes your choice"
[laughter]. You can take for your governor Eli H. Murray
or Patrick H. Lannan [applause]. I think I will take Mr.
Murray [a voice—"Don't"].

THE EDUCATION SUBTERFUGE.

Perhaps, ladies and gentlemen, I am taking up too much time [loud cries of "No, No," and "Go on"]. There is a question that has been agitating this community of late very much, especially in some quarters of this city. It is a campaign question with the conspirators. It is the educational condition of this Territory. I remember attending a political meeting held in front of the *Tribune* office on Second South Street before it removed to its present quarters. On a portion of the stand in front of the orators—it was an election subject that was on the *tapis*—was a vessel that contained a liquid to which Mr. Scott Anderson and other temperance men very much object. There was a speaker getting off the usual anti-Mormon buncombe, and as the contents of the jug grew beautifully less his articulation commenced to get proportionately thicker. He reproached the people for their alleged lack of educational facilities, and shouted "Where is your free schools? [imitating the thick articulation of the half intoxicated orator and would-be "Mormon," regenerator.] Where is your seminaries of learning?" [Laughter and applause.]

There has been on this subject a very large cat lately let out of the bag. It was the Methodists that did it this time [Laughter]. You know as well as I know that it has always been asserted that the district or common schools of Utah are sectarian, that the books used in them were sectarian or "Mormon" books; that if children of non-"Mormons" were sent there they are liable to be indoctrinated in the tenets of the "Mormon" faith. This information was conveyed to Senator Hoar by the Utah conspirators, as evinced in his speech on the Utah bill. I here have his own language, and will quote his words to show how he had been stuffed on this subject:

"We find schools established where the text books are selected wholly to instruct the youth of that community in a doctrine inconsistent, as we believe, not only with Christianity, but civilization itself."

He had been primed and loaded by the Utah calumniators of the "Mormons." But the Methodists, at a conference which lately convened at Ogden, let the whole thing out; for they considered a resolution in their meeting as to the advisibility of introducing into their denominational schools text books the same as those in use in the "'Mormon' district schools." You see they were so anxious—so deeply anxious —to have their children indoctrinated in the tenets of "Mormonism," as taught in the school books of the district schools of Utah, that they wanted to introduce them into the Methodist schools [Applause], that their pupils might all be made full-fledged "Mormons" [Applause]. This exploded the sectarian theory in relation to the district schools altogether— nothing left of it at all—and it was like all the subterfuges of the conspirators—thin as air.

Statements have frequently been made to the effect that the school-houses are inadequate, that they are mere hovels, which is not true, because we have numerous good school-houses and efficient teachers in the community, and the facilities for education, considering the age of the Territory, are commendable.

There was recently a meeting held in the 8th Ward to consider the advisability of erecting a school house, the accommodation for the school population in the 8th district being insufficient. The object of the meeting was to vote on a tax to provide means to accomplish the object in view. I should have supposed that about a quarter of an hour or so before the time of meeting the "liberal" gentlemen might have been seen rushing towards the place of meeting with their hair streaming in the wind and their coat tails in a bee-line behind them in order that they might get there in good time to vote "Aye" on the tax question, and dig deep into their pockets for the shekels to help build a new school house. I should have supposed that they would be in such a hurry to vote on the question that they could hardly be held back. But they went there and voted solid for "no tax" for school purposes. Grandly consistent! Their position on this question is like that of a man who knocks another man down, puts his foot on him, presses him hard down upon the ground, and at the same time shouts, "Why don't you get up?" [Applause.]

In the 7th Ward, on the 15th instant, a similar meeting
was held, and the gentlemen belonging to the same party
["Liberal"] were out in force. Strange to say they took the
same position as in the 8th district. And there was there in
all his glory—not a member of the district, I believe; I do
not know exactly, but I think not—Judge J. R. McBride, the
excellent and devout Methodist of a former meeting. In his
usual truthful, logical and consistent style he warned the
people that only certain persons could vote at any *election.*
You can observe the consistency and force of the remarks of
this learned gentleman, seeing that the meeting was not convened for *election* purposes at all, but to vote on the question
of whether there should be a tax imposed on the residents of
the district so as to increase its educational facilities. Every
one on the anti-Mormon side of the fence voted "No." It is
necessary to formulate another argument, now, seeing that the
sectarian one has fallen through, and it was furnished by Mr.
O. J. Hollister, ex-internal revenue collector for Utah. He
deposited his vote on that occasion on the "no tax" side of
the question. I do not deal with private matters. I deal in
public affairs, and when a man presents himself before the
public in a public capacity, then he is a subject for manipu-
lation on the public rostrum. I will give you this new reason,
furnished in two letters published subsequently to the meeting
in the *Salt Lake Herald*, from which I will quote. Listen to
what this gentleman has to say. Here is a quotation from his
communication to the *Herald:*

"It is no difference what is taught in the so-called public
schools of Utah or who teaches. The Mormon Church maintains and teaches practices that to the Gentiles are degrading
and corrupting. There is no social interchange between Mormons and Gentiles, mainly on this account. If this is the
fact as regards grown people, how much more as regards
children who cannot be expected to have much wisdom and
who are so easily contaminated and corrupted."

Here is the reason, that by the association of Gentile children with "Mormon" children the former become corrupted
by the intercourse and companionship and are degraded.
What think you of a man that would offer a premeditated

cold-blooded insult not only to every parent in the "Mormon"
Church, but to every innocent little, toddling child in that
community? What is the substance of the excuse that is
offered? It is this: "I am holier than thou." Mr. Hollister
reminds me of a character in sacred history presented by the
Savior as an illustration of the different qualities of the peti-
tions that are offered to the throne of grace. Do you remember the prayer of the self-righteous Pharisee?—"Lord I
thank thee that I am not as other men"—and let me say here,
speaking largely for other men, in this instance they are equally
thankful for the difference. [Applause.] Another argument
was made by that gentlemen on the same occasion. Here is
a quotation from another letter of his:

"I beg to reaffirm the statement and to aver, besides, that
the Gentiles have paid the full proportion of the taxes that
have built and that run the Mormon schools. * * *
The reason why the Gentiles object to paying special school
taxes besides the above, is because they cannot avail themselves of any advantage therefrom."

Here he attempts to class the "Gentiles" as anti-Mormons,
by assuming that they all feel as he and his fellow-conspira-
tors do. That is the usual trick. But let us consider
this part of the question: the Gentiles have paid their
proportion of the taxes for these purposes. O. J. Hollister was at that meeting, and so was the tax list, so I
am informed by the gentleman who took it there. And
what was on that tax list? I will tell you; the name of O. J.
Hollister conspicuous for its absence. [Applause]. This is
the position of the oracle of those who fight the school tax.

THE MORALITY SUBTERFUGE.

The "Mormons" are so very immoral according to the lies
that are formulated and spread abroad to further the interest
of the conspiracy under the popular prejudice that they may
accomplish their purposes. In the *Salt Lake Tribune,* under
date of March, 1881, there appeared a peculiar article. The
editor of the organ of the conspirators had been conversing
with a gentleman of this city on the "Mormon" question,
and this gentleman is reported in the article as stating that
he rejoiced to see the youth of the "Mormon" community

visiting drinking saloons, gambling dens, houses of ill-fame; and the editor in commenting on the remarks of this so-called gentleman, says: "if freedom can be gained without excesses, so much the better; but if not, gain the freedom, never mind the excesses." And this from the men who would regenerate the "Mormon" community. What think you of the regenerators of Utah?*

You are aware, ladies and gentlemen, that I have spoken in a similar strain as I have to-night on another occasion, quite recently, and I have in consequence been roundly abused by the organ of slander, by the organ of the conspirators; but never a word has been said in regard to my statements. None of them have been quoted or replied to. This is remarkable, because that newspaper had in that meeting a reporter. But it says: "A mentally blasted wretch, a mournful appendage of the *Deseret News*, named Nicholson [laughter], poured out his venom in the 12th Ward." Here is the argument with which I am answered. I am called "a mentally blasted wretch." [Laughter and applause.] Ladies and gentlemen, look upon me and take warning [renewed laughter and applause], and do not have the temerity at any time to fall upon the *Tribune* rock and get broken to pieces [applause]; for do you not see that the huge boulder is likely to roll over me, and, like the wheels of Juggernaut, grind me to powder? [Applause.] I have been called names; but no argument has been adduced. I have been called "a liar," an "egregious ass" [laughter] and other things too numerous to mention; but never a word of the lecture. You are capable of judging whether I am "a mentally blasted wretch" or not. [Laughter] I think I can leave the verdict in your hands.

I have been called, among other things, an alien. If there ever has been anything that I have prided myself upon it has been my birthplace, for I was born on this planet. I know no country but the earth; and I know no people but those who sustain the truth, the final triumph of which will bring about the universal brotherhood of man. I love the institutions of this country as I love my life, for they embody the principles

of human freedom; and where I find men who seek by infamous, infernal designs to crush them into the earth, I am
willing to wear myself out in their exposure. [Loud applause.]
I am not an alien, however; I am a citizen of the United
States. [Applause.] Here is the certificate [holding it up in
his hand]. Another truthful statement of the organ of the
conspirators nailed to the counter!

I have shown with some clearness I think—I hope you will
not think me egotistical if I say so—that the "Mormons" have
been defamed; that members of the community have been
murdered in cold blood and the crime has been palliated by
men who are in your midst, and who have caused lies to be
spread broadcast throughout the country. This conspiracy
has endeavored to wipe out in the Territory of Utah political
and religious freedom, that a small minority might seize the
reins of government, and despoil, and crush, and injure an
innocent community. I denounce these as crimes against
humanity; and I charge the perpetrators with being the genu-
ine agents and operators of "organized crime" in Utah. [Loud
applause.]

Thanking you for the kind attention which you have given
me, ladies and gentlemen, I wish you all a very good night.
[Loud applause.]

(A vote of thanks to the lecturer, put to the audience by
the chairman, Hon. Wm. Jennings, was carried by a shout of
"Ayes" that seemed to shake the building.)

APPENDIX.

PASSAGES FROM THE FIRST LECTURE.

IN the lecture delivered by Mr. Nicholson in the Twelfth Ward Assembly Rooms, on September 15th, the following passages occurred:

THE SLAVERY HUMBUG.

A great deal has been said about the "Mormons" being in a condition of slavery and serfdom, and these conspirators have a great deal of spmpathy for them on that account. They want to make them free; but the liberalizing process is very remarkable. They want to make them free by taking away all their political rights, and give them another kind of freedom—to visit the dens of infamy that have been established here and nurtured by them under the protest and against the active efforts of the Latter-day Saints, without a dissenting voice on their part. That is the kind of freedom they want to introduce.

But let us see how much freedom there is when you come to simmer it down in their own case. There was a man who took part in that Methodist religio-politico meeting held on the 7th of May, 1882, by the name of Jacob S. Boreman, formerly a judge of one of the judicial districts of this Territory. with his head-quarters at Beaver. There was brought up before him while he acted in that capacity a "Mormon," by the name of Alonzo Colton. He was indicted under a Territorial statute that had no reference to polygamy whatever—a Territorial law against lascivious cohabitation—and in the face of the fact that he (Boreman) knew that this statute had no application to the case, but that it ought to have come under the law of the United States against bigamy and polygamy, passed by Congress in 1862, that man was, in Jacob S. Boreman's court, convicted under the Territorial law that had no application, even if he were a polygamist. That is known and acknowledged by every man of all shades of opinion. It would be so admitted universally in this community to-day, except, perhaps, by the honorable gentleman himself. Yet he placed that man in the penitentiary through his bringing his Methodism on to the bench; and Colton served out a term of five years on a conviction brought under a law that had no application to the case. Colton's brother-in-law came up to this city some time after his incarceration. I met him several times. He drew out a petition for his release on the ground that he (Mr. Colton) was illegally convicted and unlawfully held in custody; that his conviction and imprisonment were an outrage. I saw the petition. It was taken to certain men that you and I know perfectly well—independent men who breathe the air of freedom of this great republic. But they did not sign it. They stated to the brother-in-law of Alonzo Colton, something after the language used to the "Mormons" by the late President Martin Van Buren—"Your cause is just, but I can do nothing for you." They said, in effect, that they dared not affix their signatures to that paper for fear of the *Tribune* getting after them They were so free and independent. You understand the balance. I could give you the names of those parties, but I do not wish to be too personal. This is the freedom enjoyed by the conspirators against the peace and freedom of the people of Utah.

In fact the whip of the conspirators, through their organ and the medium of public harangues, has been constantly cracked over the heads of decent men who have in the slightest manner protested against their outrageous operations against the "Mormons," until they have either been forced into line or into a silence under which they have chafed, because of the perpetual outrage upon their ideas of fair play. And yet these conspirators will talk of freedom, and talk with spread-eagle loftiness about the sweets of liberty.

THE MORALITY PLEA.

Let us enquire a little further into the comparative morality of "Mormons" and non-Mormons, as exhibited by the official statistics of two of the chief cities of Utah. In the year 1882 the total number of arrests made in Salt Lake City, by the municipal police, for crimes of every class, was 1,640; of these law-breakers 446 were "Mormons" and 1,194 non-Mormons, yet the latter constitute but one-fourth of the population. They furnished, however, three-fourths of the criminality. In 1883 the arrests amounted to 1,609 in all. Only 150 were "Mormons" and the remaining 1,459 non-Mormons.

Ogden makes a still more striking exhibit in the same direction. In 1881 the relative population was 85 per cent. "Mormons" to 15 per cent. non-Mormons. The arrests numbered 211. Of the persons arrested 21 were "Mormons," the remaining 190 being non-Mormons.

In 1882 the arrests numbered 306, the relative proportion being 22 "Mormons," to 284 non-Mormons.

In 1883 the arrests footed up 537, with a score of 74 for the lawless "Mormons" and 463 for the non-Mormons. In the last mnaed year the proportion of "Mormons" in the population was closely estimated at 71 per cent. "Mormons," leaving 29 per cent. non-Mormons.

These figures are eloquent; they speak in thunder tones, rendering comments upon their showing superfluous.

THE RESPONSIBILITY.

I might refer to cases of mobbing, and driving, and murder that have been the direct result of the publication of false statements formulated by men in this city. I was informed but yesterday by Joseph H. Parry that when he was laboring in the Southern States, in the same district where Joseph Standing was laboring, that the cause of the excitement that resulted in the death of the latter, was, that in the *Journal of Education* were published certain averments by J. M. Coyner. The cue was taken from these statements by the sectarian preachers of that region; those preachers by anti-Mormon harangues worked the people into such a frenzy that that murder was the result, and the blood spots of Joseph Standing are upon the skirts of J. M. Coyner, he being, according to Elder Parry's evidence, one of the indirect causes of that foul assassination.

STATEMENT OF R. G. McNIECE.

"It was also about eighteen months ago that our chapel and school-building in Logan was set on fire. Some one climbed in at the window and having poured coal-oil on the floor, set it on fire. The fire went out; but the next morning the burned floor and the mark of the coal-oil showed too plainly that the purpose was to burn the building."

2*

The verified facts:

"Logan, Utah, June 21, 1884.

"*Editor Deseret News:*

"I send herewith Sheriff Crookston's affidavit regarding the attempt to burn the Presbyterian church. Rev. C. M. Parks, the pastor, has made to me personally a similar statement. Mr. Parks says he will call on you on Monday next and repeat it.

"B. F. Cummings, Jr."

"Territory of Utah, County of Cache, Logan Precinct, on this 21st day of June, A. D., 1884, personally appeared before me, B. F. Cummings, Jr., a justice of the peace in and for said precinct, at my office in said precinct, Nicholas W. Crookston, who, being duly sworn, deposes and says that he is now and has been ever since before November, A. D. 1882, sheriff of Cache County.

"Said N. W. Crookston further deposes and says, 'On the morning of December 1st, A. D., 1882, I was notified that an attempt to burn the Presbyterian church in Logan had been made during the previous night. I went to the church with County Attorney Maughan. Found a quantity of kindling wood saturated with coal-oil on the floor of the bell tower. The wood had evidently been thrown there through a window and the coal-oil, afterwards found on it, from the window, and a lighted match dropped in on it. A bench used as a seat was charred, the carpet covering on it was burned and some of the kindling wood was also charred. Rev. C. M. Parks, pastor of the church, told me that on the previous evening there had been an entertainment in the church, being Thanksgiving evening; that one, Wm. Buder, came to the entertainment drunk, and that he (Parks) asked him to leave, but he (Buder) would not, and that he (Parks) then put him out by force, and that Buder then threatened to get even with him (Parks).

"'The kindling wood had been split off from round blocks sawed from a log. I took three pieces of the kindling and fitted two of them into a block which I found in Buder's yard. The way the pieces fitted, the curve of the grain, the length and the kind of wood, all proved positively that the two pieces I fitted had been split off from the log in Buder's yard. While I was fitting the piece on the block Buder came to me, took hold of me and told me to 'let that wood alone.' He seemed to be very much alarmed.

"In the month of June, A. D. 1883, Buder was in jail. I was his jailor, I told him he had better leave town, and that there was proof that he had tried to burn the Presbyterian church. In reply he said "the church didn't burn, but I'll get even with Parks before I leave town."'   N. W. Crookston.

Subscribed and sworn to before me, this 21st day of June, A. D. 1883.

B. F. Cummings, Jr.,
Justice of the Peace.

THE OLD STYLE.

To-day we print a verbatim report of an address delivered by Bishop West at Juab on the 9th inst., as forwarded by a friend.

It reads like the old-day Tabernacle harangues, and the devout brethren and sisters of the former time would have warmly enjoyed and commended it as being "full of the sperret," indeed, we are not sure but away down deep in their hearts they will approve it now. It is a very violent harangue, full of bitter malice and the usual untruths of the fanatics when they undertake to deal with subjects wherein they are opposed. The common dreary twaddle of exclusive holiness and a monopoly of honesty is disgustingly paraded by this dishonest parasite in behalf of a set of rogues whose crimes, peculations, public and private, robberies and unblushing piracies are the amazement of every one who has had to do with the facts. No spot in the Mormon administration, from the tithing yards to the county and Territorial treasuries could bear the light of day. Elder West's main insistance was, in plain words, that it was the command of the Lord, communicated through Joseph Smith, "the martyr," in a vision, about the beginning of the present month, to himself (West), that Governor Murray must be assassinated, and that his successor must in like manner be "removed," until the Gentiles were faint with terror, and let the Saints alone to manage "their own kingdom" in their own way. Of course the howling of such a noisy blatherskite in that vein simply means that he is filled with a murderous hate, but is too cowardly to himself to do the deed he undertakes to spur others up to commit. There is no danger from him, and even in the worst times the brethren had too much discretion and wholesome fear of the consequencies to undertake any such villainous programme. In former years Elder West would, however, have been sure of promotion in the church for his efforts, especially if they had been well kept up, for the sect in its wretched development of Brighamism has need of such tools. He starts in too late in the day, however, and will neither win cross, which he might have won in Jackson county, Missouri, nor crown, which he might have gained during the fanatical "reformation" which led up to the Mountain Meadow massacre.

As this notorious fabrication has created considerable interest, on account of the murderous mischief it has created, it is here published in full, as it appeared in the Salt Lake Tribune of March 15th 1884 together with a refutation of it from the pen of George Teasdale.

A RED-HOT ADDRESS.

(From the Salt Lake *Tribune*.)

Stenographical report of Bishop West's harangue in the Juab school-house, Sunday, March 9th, 1884. Reported by Tobias Tobey for the Salt Lake *Tribune*.

Juab, Utah, March 9th.

It is time, my brothers and sisters, that we ceased this cowardly silence and humble submission to the rulings and machinations of the devil and his fiery imps at the capitol of this God-forsaken Gentile government; and it is time for us to fling their defiance and scurrilous domination back in their faces. We are the elect

of Christ, and the day of judgment is at hand, and it's our turn
then if it isn't now, which I say it is. When Gabriel sounds his
trumpet on that awful day, the Gentile hellhounds will find the
Saints of God have got all the front seats reserved, and that they
can't find standing room for themselves in the gallery. The
cause is flourishing in the Juab Stake of Zion, and many souls
are being daily rescued from the flames of heathenism. If I
had my way not a house would be left standing which sheltered
a knavish Gentile. They are eyesores in the sight of the Lord
and His vengeance is sure to come. They persecute His Saints
and He has commanded them to destroy their persecutors. He
has commanded the Saints to rid the earth of the sin-besmudged
heretic. He has revealed unto us the foundation of the Gentile
Church that it is the devil. (II Nephi ch. 4, verse xx.) Hell is
filled with the scurrilous Gentiles and the floors of hell are
paved with the skulls of apostates. He who kills a Gentile rids
the earth of a serpent and adds a star to his own crown. The
Saints are gathering together from sea to sea and they will rise
in their awful might and fall upon the enemies of Zion. Let the
tabernacles resound with joyful voices for the fulfillment of the
prophecies of Moroni are at hand. The minions of the devil
are set loose in our midst by the crime soaked politicians who
rule our land. The shades of the sainted martyr Smith call
aloud for vengeance at the hands of his followers. The blood of
the Gentile persecutors shall be spilled on their own thresholds to
appease the anger of our prophet. Tune the lyre and beat the
cymbals; for our revenge is now at hand. We will wipe out the
scum of the Washington blood suckers and the high priest of
the devil who assumes to rule in our very midst shall be cut off
with a sharp instrument. The thieving Murray issues orders to
the Saints of God, and defies every one but the devil, who is
his sponsor. His head will be placed upon the walls of our city and
his entrails scattered throughout the street of Zion, that every
Gentile adventurer may behold and take a care that we are left
to pursue our road to Paradise unmolested. Our strength is
greater than the world believes and our will is powerful and
undaunted by heretic menaces. The Lord is our shepherd and
we cannot fail. The red man is our firm ally and he thirsts for
the blood of the enemy of Zion. We are powerful and unassail-
able in our mountain home and we will roll the massive boulders
of destruction down from the mountain tops upon the heads of
the unregenerate. Our secret places are stored with crafty explo-
sives with which we will surely destroy the strongholds of the
government of Satan. Our young men are drilling for the
conflict, and our wives and daughters are making themselves
ready to minister to our wants, and the day is close at hand.
Let the Gentile leeches and poltroons beware and win our for-
bearance, if yet they may. The Lord is sorely angered at our
persecutors, and He has said to our counselors in a vision that
He will deliver our enemy into our hands as He delivered Laban
into the hands of Nephi. He will visit the earth, through us,
with a worse destruction than He did in the days of the flood,
and the ungodly will bite the dust with rage, and their blood
will flow in the streets of Zion even as much as the waters in the

day of Noah. Behold, I declare unto you, all ye Saints who revere the memory of the Prophets, that you must begin to gird up your loins and whet your knives. Let the religious fervor of the Saints who are dead and gone recur to your weaker spirits and fire you with the zeal of the destroying angels. Eli Murray is the Cain of our generation. He hates our people and he works for our destruction that he may win for himself a reputation of valor among the ungodly. He is a damned scoundrel, and a pestiferous leper. He is the polluted scum of corruption. He reeks with ungodliness, and he is rotten with heresy. I command every true disciple of Christ to watch out for this damned Yankee interloper, and ye know that there is protection enough for you in Zion if ye kill the whole Gentile race. Last night, as I lay in my bed thinking over the affairs of the Church, and possessed of a strange restlessness, and praying the while for inspiration from the Most High, that I might see the way more clearly to a sure release of my brethren from bondage, behold a great and glorious light suddenly filled my apartment with a glow brighter than the sun. I was at first afraid, and inclined strongly to leap from my bed and flee. But of a sudden I heard a voice which caused my heart to beat with tumultuous joy, for it was that of Joseph Smith. I gazed at him earnestly, expecting and hanging on the words which should perchance fall from his lips, and I beheld that his garments were of a dazzling whiteness, and that his skin was of a dazzling and heavenly whiteness, save the blood-red spots and livid wounds where the bullets of the cursed Gentiles had entered his sainted body, and which were now visible to their eternal damnation, as were the marks of the nails which pierced the hands and feet of Christ. Joseph spoke to me in a voice of wondrous sweetness blended with strains of the direst severity when he spoke of the fate in store for those Saints who neglected what he should now command them. Joseph bade me to cast my eyes about and behold the presence in the midst of the Saints of an emissary of the devil. It was the will of the Most High that this man should be removed, and if other emissaries were chosen to fill his place, even as many as were so chosen should be similarly dealt with. If allowed to remain in our midst, the sin would be on our heads, for it was the command of the Most High God of Abraham and Isaac. It lay in our power to be our own rulers, and our cowardice was the cause of sore distress to the departed Saints who had left us a kingdom. Eli H. Murray was possessed of a devil, and had only the outward semblance of a man. He should and must be trod upon until his bowels gushed out in the streets. The incarnate fiend lurked invisibly behind his hellish disciple, and was intent upon the destruction of Zion. The time was short, and vigorous and immediate action premptory The curses of eternal damnation awaited those who failed in this holy mission. The work must not stop at the destruction of one of these hell-hounds, these Erebus-like pestilences in the folds of the anointed, but must extend even to the furthermost corners of the earth, until every heretic out of hell was sent home, and the Latter-day Saints were rulers of the land. Much more the beloved Joseph said to me which I am commanded not to reveal unto you until you prove the sincerity of your faith and love for the prosperity of Zion from what has already been revealed. The direst plagues shall be immediately visited upon you and your children if these divine commands go unheeded. I call upon you who sit there trembling in your seats to beware, and to rise in your strength and win your crown. Let every Saint in Zion be present at the meeting in this building on Sunday next at this hour, and I will discourse further upon these matters which I have, for wise reasons, kept from you during the day up to this minute. The Lord bless you. Amen.

THE FOUL LIBEL REFUTED.

NEPHI, JUAB CO., U. T.

March 18, 1884.

Editor Deseret News:

Please pardon me for referring to a sheet published in your city, called the "Salt Lake *Tribune*," although I do not presume that it is sustained by any respectable person in this Territory where it has so unenviable a reputation; still it may be sent abroad and fall into the hands of some simple-minded persons who might perhaps be deluded into the impression that it was a truthful sheet, or reliable authority. Not that I think for a moment that any sane person would be so woefully deceived. I wish to refer to a manufactured sensational piece in the issue of Sunday the 16th inst.. that has been called to my attention, headed a "Red-Hot Address;" also a short editorial on the subject in which the truthful (?) editor states it had been "forwarded by a friend." *O, tempore! O, mores!* It purports to be a "stenographical report of Bishop West's harangue in the Juab schoolhouse, Sunday March 9, 1884, reported by 'Tobias Tobey' for the Salt Lake *Tribune*." Then follows an address which charity would suggest had been written by an insane person or worse, the offspring of a dreadfully corrupt heart, a miserable disgrace to the *genus homo*, worthy only to rise to "shame' and everlasting contempt."

Now, the facts are these: It is all a gross fabrication. Juab is a small town occupied by hotel and boarding house keepers, a store or two and the railroad hands; there is a small branch of the Church, presided over by Elder James Wilson. who is very much respected, but no bishop. On the Sunday referred to there had been a wash-out and all the hands were busy, so that there was no meeting held on that day; and as far as the "Bishop West" is concerned, there is no such bishop there or in the "Mormon" Church, and who "Tobias Tobey" is no one knows.

I have been requested to inform you of these facts, and kindly request that you will waive any feeling of dislike you may have to, in any way, refer to the existence of such a sheet, for the sake of our young Elders on missions, who might perchance meet with this shockingly vile fabrication.

Very Respectfully,

GEORGE TEASDALE.

WHAT UTAH WANTS.

The Salt Lake *Tribune* of March 6th, 1881, had an editorial headed, "What Utah Wants," from which we make the following extracts:

"Apropos of the new and petty war recently started by the municipal government on the women of the town, the liquor dealers and the gambling fraternity, one of the 'enemy' said to us the other day: 'It may be a hard thing to say, and perhaps harder still to maintain, but I believe that billiard halls, saloons and houses of ill-fame are more powerful reforming agencies here in Utah than churches and schools, or even than the *Tribune.* What the youug Mormons want is to be freed. So long as they are slaves, it matters not much to what or to whom, they are and they can be nothing. Your churches are as enslaving as the Mormon Church. Your party is as bigoted and intolerant as the Mormon party. At all events I rejoice when I see the young Mormon hoodlums playing billiards, getting drunk, running with bad women—anything to break the shackles they were born in, and that every so-called religious or virtuous influence only makes the stronger. Some of them will go quite to the bad, of course, but it is better so, . for they are made of poor stuff, and since there is no good reason why they were begun for let them soon be done for, and the sooner the better. Most of them, however, will soon weary of vice and dissipation, and be all the stronger for the knowledge of it and of its vanity. At the very least they will be free, and it is of such vital consequence that a man should be free, that in my opinion his freedom is cheáply won at the cost of some familiarity with low life. And while it is not desirable in itself, it is to me tolerable, because it appears to offer the only inducement strong enough to entice men out of slavery into freedom.'

So far, the *Tribune's* pretended quotation. Now for its own comments, in the same article:

"*Freedom is the first requisite of manhood, and if it can be won without excesses so much the better. If it can't, never mind the excesses, win the freedom.* It is not you who are responsible, when it comes to that; it is those who have enslaved you. Who is the national hero of the yeomanry of England but Robin Hood, 'waging war against the men of law, against bishops and archbishops, whose sway was so heavy; generous, moreover; giving a poor, ruined knight clothes, horse and money to buy back the land he had pledged to a rapacious Abbott; compassionate, too, and kind to the poor, enjoining his men not to injure yeomen and laborers, but above all rash, bold, proud, who would go to draw his bow before the sheriff's eyes and to his face; ready with blows, whether to give or take.'

*   *   *   *   *   *

"Read the first chapter of Book Two of Taine's English Literature, if you would see what ails Utah, and what it needs as a medicament."

"To vent the feelings, to satisfy the heart and eyes, to set free boldly on all the roads of existence, the pack of appetites and instincts, this was the craving which the manners of the time betrayed. It was 'merry England,' as they called it then. It was not yet stern and constrained. It expanded widely, freely, and rejoiced to find itself so expanded."

*   *   *   *   *

"Let the people of Utah rise out of the dust, stand upright, inquire within, lean on themselves, look about them, and try in a large way to be men, as they were born to be. Let them know nobody more puissant than themselves. What is a game of billiards, a glass of beer, a cup of coffee, cigar, or other petty vice, in the span of a strong human life, filled with endeavor in the right direction? The Territory, like the rest of the land, is still in in its infancy, still in the pulp of babyhood. It has yet to be made. There is work for men, whose first and last quality is strength. manliness. The day of trifles, and of crouching and cowardice, of criminal surrender to the first howling dervish who calls himself a priest and presumes to speak in the name of the Almighty, has lasted long enough. Let a new era dawn in which men shall dare to be men."